# SOME ONE TO LOVE ME

## ABC'S OF LOVE

**JUANITA JONES**

authorHOUSE

*AuthorHouse™*
*1663 Liberty Drive*
*Bloomington, IN 47403*
*www.authorhouse.com*
*Phone: 833-262-8899*

*Published by AuthorHouse  02/15/2023*

*ISBN: 979-8-8230-0085-7 (sc)*
*ISBN: 979-8-8230-0084-0 (e)*

*Print information available on the last page.*

*This book is printed on acid-free paper.*

*Scripture taken from the King James Version of the Bible.*

A: Love is Amazing

B: Love is Beautiful

C: Loving is Caring

D: Love is Devoted

E: Love is Enjoying

F: Love is Forgiving

G: Love is God

H: Love is Happiness

I: Love is Inspiring

J: Love is Joyful

K: Love is Kind

L: Love is Loyalty

M: Love is Motivation

N: Love is Necessary

O: Love is Open Heart to Love

P: Love is Priceless

Q: Love is the Quality of Love

R: Love is Rewarding

S: Love is Sharing

T: Love is Trust

U: Love is Unfailing

V: Love is Valuable

W: Love is Worthwhile

X: Love is the X-factor in life

Y: Love is Youthful and Young at Heart

Z: Love is the Zest of Life

# Someone to love me, author Juanita Jones

Love is the epitome of God's grace and divine protection. The love of God and grace of God has protected me from unseen as well as seen dangers. Embarking upon love and being loved, reminded me of the times that I spent with my grandmother, who was the Matriarch of the family. A strong Godly pillar of strength, wisdom, love, and a powerful prayer intercessor that would pray without ceasing. She would love you through the good and bad times. I went to church with my grandmother on a regular basis. We would walk to church and her deacon would give us a ride back home. Grandmother's favorite words and routine would be "Go to the bathroom now because you will not distract the Pastor by going back and forth" and "Don't talk to other children while the Pastor is preaching; respect God and the House of God because it is very disrespectful."

My mother was a hard-working woman, an awesome cook, and an amazing baker. I loved her homemade butter pound cake. She was also a disciplinarian and believed in the power of the belt. My dad loved me and basically allowed me to do whatever I wanted with certain restrictions. As a young girl, growing up and maturing, my parents were overprotective. One day, my dad was talking to me about the birds and the bees. As he started, I could see and feel the uncomfortable emotions displayed on his face and in his voice. Dad would say, "When you see that devil, leave him alone!" Well, at a young tender age, as a young woman looking for love and to be loved by a man, how do you define the devil? He was my very first example of how a man is supposed to treat a woman. My dad loved me but never spent enough time with me. I only wished that he had invested more time.

I know what it is to desire and fantasize about love and falling in love. I had to learn the difference when someone loved me but was not 'in love' with me. I made excuses about why I shouldn't be loved because of the pain of rejections, insecurities, disappointments and being mishandled by those that I loved but didn't love me. I have made others a priority whereas I was only an option. Growing up, I never learned how to love myself, I was too busy catering and loving others faithfully. I encountered false hope and uncommitted relationships based on lies and betrayal. I decided to put relationships on hold until God sent the man that He created for me. God's timing is perfect! During that time, I did not know that I was looking for love in all the wrong places. If we are all honest and transparent, at some time or another, we have all looked for love in the wrong places and in the wrong people. It may come from a forbidden friendship, unstable relationship, or companion.

I encountered a lot in my life, but I came to the realization that it was my grandmother's prayers that got me through many heartbreaks. My grandmother prayed for me and always pointed me in the direction of God. Her legacy was, "Have faith in God and serve God to the best of your ability". These are the words that she left me, "No matter what you go through, Trust God and don't let go of God's hand; hold on baby, to God's word." My grandmother lived to be 100 years old, no Dementia or Alzheimer's or wheelchair, just a cane because her knees were a little weak and she needed to balance herself. At 100 years old, grandmother continued to go to church until her health began to decline. However, her mind was sharp and clear. I watched my grandmother go into her eternal sleep and once again my heart was broken.

As I struggled with the very thought to love and be loved, I poured all my love into my son, granddaughters, and family. As I pondered on the thought to love and be loved, a unique, peaceful, and soothing voice spoke to me with such an undeniable love filled with great compassion that I never experienced before. It said, "Daughter, I love you with an endless love, I fell in love with you in my mind before I created you. You are my masterpiece." It reflected upon my situations and circumstances that only God could have brought me out. Failed relationships, betrayal of a friend, deemed as an outcast, rejection from the very people that I loved, but didn't love me. God is love. At that moment, I felt the love that I so desired and what I was looking for. He was there all the time. I wasn't aware of it because I was busy loving and catering to others, that I didn't take the time to love myself and accept God's unconditional love.

Someone To Love Me was God loving me beyond measure. God was always there through the good, bad and ugly. God validated me. I am loved, I am healed, I am royalty, and I am more than enough.

I am who God says I am. That's more than enough for me.

# Dedication

Special dedication to the Author and Finisher of my Faith, my Lord & Savior Jesus Christ.

My Mother, Florrie E. Jones
My Beloved Son, De'Shawn Jones
My Granddaughters, Tee' Mone, Ivoriona, Sharionna
Loving Niece, Antoinette L. Belton
Overseer: Bishop Eric Fiatti
Apostle Patricia Middleton
Apostle Samantha Stewart-Sunkins
Pastor Faith Washington
Apostle George Washington
Apostle Mary Ann Frazier
Prophet Joel Redmond
Juanita Bobian
La'Tarsha Jones Williams
Angelena Jones Murray
Lahoma Scott

*I would like to dedicate this book to everyone*
*that is looking for love, hope to love,*
*or expecting to embrace love and expectations of love.*

*I want you to know that God loves you with endless love.*

**His love never fails.**

# Acknowledgment

*A very special thank you to Dr. Samantha Stewart-Sunkins for prophesying this book into existence during the year of 2019 at the Daughters of Destiny Women's Conference. Thanks for pushing me toward my destiny, undergirding me with prayers, love, and encouragement to write this book ordained by God.*

*Thank you, Author Clarisa C.J. Hyson, Elder Etrenda Ferguson, Prophetess Pamela Logan Battiste, Author Wendye Savage and Recording Artist Saundra Woods for your prayers and support.*

*I appreciate your endless motivation to launch me forward in completing this book.*

# Foreword

## PASTOR FAITH WASHINGTON

It has been a pleasure knowing Juanita Jones for over ten plus years and being able to see and feel the love of God demonstrated through her towards so many people.

To show the love that Juanita has while seeking for love, speaks volumes and shows the inner strength that she was ordained to share.

Congratulations to you, Juanita Jones on your first book and may you continue to display the love of God through your everyday living.

# Table of Contents

Introduction ................................................................xix

Chapter 1:   What is Love?................................................ 1

Chapter 2:   Why Do We Desire Love? .......................... 3

Chapter 3:   The Expressions of Love ............................ 5

Chapter 4:   Love Heals................................................... 7

Chapter 5:   The Impact of Love.................................... 9

Chapter 6:   Love Speaks................................................11

Chapter 7:   The Languages of Love..............................13

Chapter 8:   The Gift of Love ........................................17

Chapter 9:   Walk in Love ..............................................19

Chapter 10: Love Forgives..............................................21

Chapter 11: The Courage to Love ..................................23

Chapter 12: Love Never Fails .........................................25

Chapter 13: Types of Love and What they Mean ..........27

Chapter 14: God's Love Letter........................................29

# Introduction

This book was preordained by God. It was confirmed by Prophesy through the Holy Spirit by the Servant of the most-high God, Dr. Samantha Stewart-Sunkins. This book entitled, 'Someone to Love Me' was produced out of pains, rejections, frustrations, being misunderstood, insecurities, and loneliness with a desire to be loved.

I was dwelling in thought about love and to be loved. A unique, soothing, and sweet voice filled with undeniable peace, joy, compassion, and love that I never knew or experienced in my life spoke to me and said, "Daughter, I loved you before I went to the drawing board to personally design you. I fell in love with you in my mind before I created you."

"My beautiful daughter, you were wonderfully and marvelously created. I knew your height, weight, facial features, color, and DNA before you were born. I am God, the creator of all flesh. I even knew the mistakes that you were going to make, the wrong choices and decisions when it came to love, before you made them, and I forgave you."

I've never stopped loving you because my love towards you is unconditional and I consider you to be my masterpiece. My Servant, David, was the apple of my eyes, even when he sinned.

With Bathsheba, I never stopped loving David, I loved him with an endless love.

I knew David's heart and his authentic love towards me; he was a man after my heart.

True love knows forgiveness and that is the birthing place of healing.

Love keeps no record of wrongs."

# Chapter One

## WHAT IS LOVE?

Love is defined as a deep affection for another person. Love also means to feel this intense affection for someone. However, everyone's definition of love is very different; it all depends on the individual and their concept or definition of love.

Someone's definition of love may be based on personality, attraction, sexual desires, or the need to be cared for or comforted. While others seek companionship to avoid loneliness.

To be loved is the unwavering confidence of unselfishness. True commitment to love is fortified with forgiveness through the good, bad, and ugly. Love is sharing without hesitation or regrets. Love is loving so deeply, it's not an option, but a priority.

The soothing effect of authentic love is laughter, expressions of unspeakable joy. Love is not a fairy tale, but the transcendent of God Agape's love for you. God is Love.

### READ- *1 Corinthians 13:4-5*

# Chapter Two

## WHY DO WE DESIRE LOVE?

There is a built-in hard drive, a maternal (internal) implant to (love and be loved.) When God created you in His image, you were so special and near to God's heart that He designed your fingerprint uniquely to distinguish you from everyone else; no one can be duplicated.

### We love because God first loved us.

God loves you so much, He was willing to make the ultimate sacrifice, His only begotten son, Jesus, (The Christ. God's blueprint of love was placed in. Therefore, your internal instinct is to love and be loved because we were created out of love.

Love not only makes the world go around, but it's also worth the ride. When a mother conceived and carried her baby for nine months, the morning sickness, swollen feet, birthing pain that is associated with pregnancy does not compare to the bundle of joy after seeing her baby; love at first sight. The journey of bonding between mother and child begins.

We desire love and to be loved because God placed that desire within us. Love creates and does not destroy. Love is a constructed force to rebuild and rebirth and not abort. Love is the driving force behind forgiveness and healing. God's love is endless and authentic.

*Read: 1 John 4:16*

# Chapter Three

## THE EXPRESSIONS OF LOVE

My love for you is unconditional and eternal.

You bring the best out in me.

Love is like listening to my favorite song, emerging me with the desire to dance all night long with you.

Love speaks from the heart. There is no hidden agenda or motive. Expressions of love begin with you.

Love yourself.

Be the best version of you.

Rock your own world.

The expression of authentic love is not expressed in words, but through acts of kindness, giving and sacrifices. God so loved the world that He gave His only begotten son, Jesus. Love is expressed in acts to do something kind and helpful for another person. Perhaps your time or giving your undivided attention. Love expresses that you are not an option but a priority in someone's life.

Love can be expressed through gifts. In fact, love is a gift. Love takes off the mask and allows you to be seen as who God created you to be. You are not a carbon copy of someone else. I love you for who you are, not who you pretend to be.

*Read: 1 Corinthians: 16:14*

*Juanita Jones*

# Chapter Four

## LOVE HEALS

Love heals when we choose to forgive those that deliberately choose to do us wrong, afflict or hurt us. To be healed is to let it go and embrace the freedom to release the power over you by harboring unforgiveness, bitterness and holding on to your pain.

You may cause internal illnesses as well as emotional unbalance or stagnation. Love promotes growth, changes and a healthy and balanced life of peace and joy. God is love. His love brings healing to the mind, spirit, and soul. God heals the broken hearted and binds the wounds along with the freedom to love again and the desire to continue to love.

Peace, I leave with you. My peace, I give unto not as the world giveth. Love heals when we choose to forgive and love others. Love has the power to forgive. In fact, love has the ability to heal the world.

*Read: Jeremiah 30:17*

# Chapter Five

## THE IMPACT OF LOVE

Love promotes emotional and mental well-being. Love reduces anxiety and stress. Love is a powerful tool for motivation that can affect you both physically, mentally, and emotionally.

The impact of love shows affection, displays acts of kindness, compassion, reciprocates loving gestures, prioritizes spending time with one another, and being willing to forgive and apologize when you are wrong or make a mistake.

Recognize and acknowledge the authenticity of love based on true commitment. The impact of love is stronger than death.

Psalm 94:18-19

# Chapter Six

## LOVE SPEAKS

Love is a language everyone can speak and express. Love will speak the truth and not lie. Love speaks through gifts; taking the time and effort to actually buy someone a gift, even if it's big or small. These gifts do not have to be expensive, it is simply the mere facts that you thought about the person, a matter of the heart.

Love speaks through kind acts of service such as: giving a person a ride, grocery shop for them, etc. This type of 'acts of love' do not go unnoticed, it speaks volume. Language speaks through a physical touch, a smile, a hug, and merely holding someone's hand and reminding them that you are here for them and that you care.

Sometimes it only takes only a 'touch' and love can leave an imprint in one's heart. Fashion yourself after the love of God. It will lift you up when any and everything tries to demote you. Love will lift the load when the weight seems impossible to carry the weight. Love will inspire you NOT to give up.

*Read: Ephesians 3:20-4*

# *Chapter Seven*

## THE LANGUAGES OF LOVE

The language of love is expressed and spoken in different languages:

1. **English: I love you**
   *Where it's spoken: United States, Canada, United Kingdom, Austria, Singapore and the*
   *Pacific Islands.*

2. **Spanish: Te amo, Te quiero**
   *Where it's spoken: Spain, Equatorial, Guinea, United States, Pacific Islands*

3. **French: Je t'aime**
   *Where it's spoken: Belgium, (Wallonia, Brussels, Canada, Quebec, France, Switzerland, French, Caribbean, French Polynesia, Francophone, Africa*

4. **German: Ich liebe Dich**
   *Where it's spoken: Austria, Germany, Switzerland, Belgium*

5. **Italian: ti amo**
   *Where it's spoken: Italy, Switzerland, San Marino*

6. **Russian: yatebya liubliu**
   *Where it's spoken: Russia, Mongolia, Soviet Union*

7. **Ukrainian: yo tebe kokhayu**
   *Where it's spoken: Ukraine*

8. **Arabic: ahabak**
   *Where it's spoken: North Africa, Western Asia (Middle East), East Africa*

9. **Greek: s'agapo**
   *Where it's spoken: Greece, Cyprus*

10. **Afrikoans: El jet joulief**
    *Where it's spoken: South Africa*

11. **Hebrew:** (Man to Woman) ani ohev otach
    (Woman to Man) ani ohevet otach
    (Woman to Woman) ani ohevet otcha
    (Man to Man) ani ohev otcha
    *Where it's spoken: Israel*

12. **Hungarian: Szeretlek**
    *Where it's spoken: Hungary, Area's in Neighboring Countries*

13. **Swedish: Jag alskar dig**
    *Where it's spoken: Sweden, Finland*

14. **Haitian Creole: mwen renmen w**
    *Where it's spoken: Haiti*

15. **Turkish: Seni seviyorum**
    *Where it's spoken: Turkey, Cyprus, Bulgaria*

16. **Dutch: ik hou van jou**
    Where it's spoken: Belgium, (Flanders, Brussels), Netherlands

17. **Polish: Kocham, Cie**
    Where it's spoken: Poland, Germany, United Kingdom, Western Ukraine, USA, Belarus

18. **Vietnamese: anh Yeuem**
    *Where it's spoken: Vietnam*

19. **Japanese: Ya lyublyu tebya**
    *Where it's spoken: Japan*

20. **Portuguese: Cute amo**
    *Where it's spoken: Portugal, Brazil, Mozambique, Angola, Guinea-Bissau, East Timor, Equatorial Guinea*

# Chapter Eight
## THE GIFT OF LOVE

Love cannot be bought or sold

Love is Priceless

Love is Valuable

Love is Kind

Love is the tranquil of peace that electrifies
throughout your very inner being

Love doesn't discriminate but love integrates

Love is giving without leaving one's (you) bankrupt

The essence of love is unselfishness

The ability to love yourself is intimately related
to your capacity to love others

The gift of love is a gift from God freely given unconditionally

*Read: John 3:16*

*Some One to Love Me*

# Chapter Nine

## WALK IN LOVE

To walk in love, we must first be willing to walk out of some things such as unforgiveness, bitterness, envy and gravitate toward forgiveness.

We must be imitators of God (Christ). To be imitators of God means that we must Imitate His love.

There is no greater expression of love than God. God is Love. God's love is a sustainer, He will sustain and provide for you. God will meet you where you are; He loves you just that much!

God's delight in comforting His children. God expects us to love and walk in love because that is the proof that you know God.

Everything that God does is out of love. Love never gives up or loses.

Walk in love and you will attract God's blessings to yourself. Love is the gateway to Heaven.

*Read: Ephesian 5:2*

# Chapter Ten

## LOVE FORGIVES

Love is the most powerful tool of forgiveness and God will give you the power to forgive. God shows His love for us while we were still sinners. Christ died for us, so we are to forgive others if we are to forgive others if we wish to be forgiven.

There is no love without forgiveness. Forgiveness is the epitome of love. Love does not masquerade in unforgiveness.

The person that gains the most from forgiveness is the person that does the giving. Love restores and covers a multitude of sins. Love holds no record of unforgiveness.

*Read: Ephesians 4:32 KJV*

# Chapter Eleven

## THE COURAGE TO LOVE

After a breakup, betrayal, divorce, or fear in a relationship, you may dwell on the thought of whether you should give love another chance to love and be loved. It may be hard to have the courage to love again, or to allow someone to love you. Everyone at some point desires love in a natural or physical way. To be loved is to allow someone to love you authentically with no hidden motives or agenda.

The heart of the matter is to be accepted for who you are, not an unrealistic thought of who you perceive that a person should be. The courage to love again is not allowing past experiences to affect your ability to love and be loved. Allowing God to send the very man or woman that He created and especially designed for you. Love knows no fear. Forgive wholeheartedly. Sometimes we hold on to things that God wants us to let go; receive your freedom.

At one time or another, we look for love in the wrong places. When God wants you to wait for the right person, it will be ordained by Him in all the right places. "The Courage to Love" is to accept love and be loved and know that you are worthy to be loved because 'You know who you are and know that you are loved by God'. We are created in His image and God fell in love with (you) in His mind before He went to the drawing board to design you. You are His masterpiece. He gives the courage to love again.

*Read: John 4:8*

*Some One to Love Me*

# Chapter Twelve

## LOVE NEVER FAILS

The love of God will never fail. The very nature of God is love. His love promotes Grace and Mercy, and it endures all things no matter what you encounter or go through. God's love will see you through because love endures all things.

God is eternal; therefore, His love will last throughout all eternity. God loves you with an everlasting love. Love is patient and kind. Love does not envy or boast; it is not arrogant or rude. It does not exist on its own, and it is not irritable or resentful or rejoice at wrongdoings, but it rejoices within the truth.

No matter what you do in life, if your motives are not right, it means absolutely nothing.

*Read: 1 Corinthians: 13:4-8*

# *Chapter Thirteen*

## *TYPES OF LOVE AND WHAT THEY MEAN*

**Agape:** Selfless universal love. Agape love is a 'one of a kind' love. It is an empathetic, selfless love for others that includes a love for God and love for mankind.

**Eros:** Romantic, passionate love.

**Storage:** Unconditional love, familial love that refers to the love of parents for their children. It is a protective kinship based love.

**Phila:** Affectionate, friendly love. Philia is a friendly love shared between friends and family members characterized by loyalty and trust.

**Ludus:** Playful, flirtatious, non-committed relationship. Ludus means having a crush on someone, no strings attached; a playful game.

**Pragma:** Committed long lasting relationship, built on endurance and commitment.

**Philautia:** Self-love. Recognize your self-worth and do not ignore yourself or personal needs.

1 Corinthians :13: 4-8

# Chapter Fourteen

## GOD'S LOVE LETTER

Dear My Love:

I have loved you from the beginning of time. I created you in my very image and my love will not compare to another. The depth of my love for you is incomprehensible. My love never fails.

My love corrects in truth. You are the apple of my eyes. My delight in you reflects my love for you.

You hold the keys to my heart. My love for you is like a burning torch that cannot be put out.

Whenever you feel alone and feel that no one cares, simply cast your cares upon me. I care and love you with endless love. My love is everlasting. I love you throughout eternity.

You are my love child that was created in my image and out of authentic love. You are my masterpiece so take a bow, my love child.

You are my rainbow in the sky. I poured my love into your heart.

### GOD

# *Prayer*

Most Holy and Everlasting Father; thank you for your unwavering and unconditional love. Thank you for the peace that compasses all understanding. I stand in awe of your desire to love me despite all my mistakes and faults. You recognize my needs and supply all of them according to your richness and glory in Christ Jesus.

Thank you, Father, for empowering me to be who you created me to be, a reflection of your love and glory.

When I was unable to speak, you spoke for me. When I was unable to walk, you carried me. When I was discouraged, you encouraged me. Thank you for being there for me and being that "Someone to Love Me".

Help me to fulfill my earthly assignment so I can put a smile on your face. May I forever follow in your footsteps and love others unconditionally as you have loved me.

In Jesus name, I pray. I decree and declare that it is so.

So be it.

# Someone to Love Me

Do you have the courage to love again?
(Fill in the blank)

---
---
---
---
---
---
---
---
---
---
---
---
---
---
---
---
---
---
---
---
---
---
---
---
---
---
---

# Someone to Love Me

Notes

_____

_____

_____

_____

_____

_____

_____

_____

_____

_____

_____

_____

_____

_____

_____

_____

_____

_____

_____

_____

_____

_____

_____

_____

_____

_____

_____

# About the Author

Juanita Jones is a native of South Carolina. She graduated from Lahairo Bible University, Augusta, Georgia and studied at Beaufort Technical College. Juanita has worked in the medical field for over thirty years as a Medical Certified Nursing Attendant.

Juanita Jones serves as a powerful prayer intercessor under the leadership of Apostle Patricia Middleton and Overseer Bishop Eric Fiatti.

She is a loving mother of De'Shawn T. Jones and a dedicated grandmother of three adorable granddaughters; Tee'Mone, Ivoriona and Sharionna Jones.

**Juanita believes that with GOD, all things are possible.**

# References

Bishop Michael Curry: Love is the way

Author Elizabeth Rider: 7 Types of Love

Holy Bible: King James Version

Printed in the United States
by Baker & Taylor Publisher Services